The Little Red Chicken
&
The Big Alligator

Written by Gilroy Barrett &

Rasta Reuben Kwabena

Illustrated by Omar Taylor

Copyright © 2024

All Rights Reserved

The Little Red Chicken & The Big Alligator

Written by Gilroy Barrett & Rasta Reuben Kwabena

Illustrated by Omar Taylor

Livications

(Gilroy Kirk Barrett)

To my two children, Jodian and Dorilee, they were the first ones who read the story and let me know that it's good.

So, they gave me the encouragement and the confidence to go forward now and publish this storybook for children.

To my Grandma Vida Richards,

who is always telling those old Jamaican folk stories about life.

I have learned a lot from you in this way,

and your stories have helped to spark my imagination.

Thanks for your unconditional love and prayers.

Livications

(Rasta Reuben Kwabena)

Livicated to all the children and grandchildren, and all the relatives and friends of the Great Jamaican Grandmother Amber.

And for all the families and children of the world to enjoy the joyful journey of reading and learning.

To inspire and spark creative imagination within the great tradition of storybooks and children's education.

Big respect to all the Grandmothers and Grandfathers who often teach the young generation with stories and songs. And with clever sayings of parables and words of wisdom.

Acknowledgments

(Gilroy Kirk Barrett)

Special Thanks to My Mom for being there for me from the day of my birth up until now. Thanks for supporting and encouraging me and always telling me never to give up on my dreams.

Also, thanks to my wife for her great support over these years.

To all my family members, whom I have not mentioned by name, thank you all for your support.

And Big Thanks to my co-author (Rasta Reuben Kwabena). Your creative writing style is truly complimentary to the telling of the story. Thanks for enhancing my story and for helping to bring the vision alive. Thanks for believing in me and my writing skills. It's an honour to work with you on this project and many more to come.

Great thanks to the illustrator, Omar Taylor; you did a very good job telling the story in your own unique style of colourful and expressive artwork. And as the saying goes, these pictures speak more than a thousand words.

Acknowledgments
(Rasta Reuben Kwabena)

The gift of creative imagination comes from the power of creation and the power of Mother Nature. I am thankful and grateful to Jah Most High for gifting us talent and inspiration.

This story is based upon an idea by Mr. Gilroy Barrett. I am happy and honoured to work together with you, as co-authors in teamwork and unity. To help bring forth this brilliant storybook idea from dream to reality. Thanks for recognizing my talent in the field of creative writing. Great minds think alike, and good teamwork makes the dream work.

Special thanks to Iness Karola for all your help and encouragement along the way. Thanks for helping us diligently with the editing & proofreading for this storybook project to complete the text with correct grammar and proper punctuation, etc. Big thanks to my mother & father. And thanks to all the mothers and children in The Great Amber Family in Jamaica and around the world. Thanks for encouraging my creative journey from the early days up to the present. And thanks to all my brothers and sisters and all the good teachers and good friends who helped me along the way to prepare for success today.

About The Story

The story of the Little Red Chicken is a cleverly written, inspiring and intriguing children's story. It is both educational and entertaining, with lots of fun and adventure for the entire family. Highlighting good moral teachings for children and their families, such as learning to understand the importance of caution and the power of courage. And learning to respect and honour the great value of parental advice and good guidance.

This children's storybook takes the reader on a playful journey. Stepping into the world of the Little Red Chicken as she journeys along her way to find a safe place to play. Along the way in this adventure, she meets a Big Alligator, and she learns about being responsible and careful. She learns to honour and treasure the guiding words of her mother's teachings. And most of all, she learns the true value of caution and the power of courage.

This storybook inspires children to enjoy outdoor activities and have fun in the sun. To appreciate nature, to admire and respect the kingdom of the animals and the birds of the air. The main character of the story is a brave and smart Little Red Chicken. She is playful and outspoken, confident, adventurous, and beautiful. She is not afraid to spread her wings and fly, and she is not afraid to take a chance and try. And even if she fails, she is not afraid to try again.

She is strong and bold, and she loves to take action. To participate in the beauty of the outdoors and to enjoy the wonderful world of nature.

The Little Red Chicken is a highly motivated creative thinker who believes in standing up for herself. She doesn't let anything worry or bother her even though she knows what it means to be on the top of the food chain! Still, she is independent and fearless, with a joyful heart and a funny sense of humour.

Protecting herself with bravery, cleverness, and charisma. The story of the Little Red Chicken is filled with skillful rhymes and parables of wisdom, smartly written into the narrative of the unfolding story. Revealing major life lessons for children and the entire family.

The Little Red Chicken & The Big Alligator

Written by Gilroy Barrett & Rasta Reuben Kwabena

Illustrated by Omar Taylor

Once upon a time,
there was a Little Red Chicken
who wanted to cross the pond to get to the other side.
But the Little Red Chicken could not swim nor fly. And there was no way for the Little Red Chicken to walk around the pond, to get to the other side, because the pond was so big, and it was so wide.

With a tearful look in her eyes,
The Little Red Chicken looked across the water.
And she looked up high into the sky. Oh, she wished that she could swim, and oh, she wished that she could fly.

In the middle of the pond, there lived a big, hungry alligator that was always swimming around and splashing in the water.

He looked like he was smiling and grinning with his big alligator teeth. But he was just floating up and down the pond, looking around and croaking for food to eat.

When the Big Alligator saw the Little Red Chicken, he started daydreaming about cooking in the kitchen.

Thinking, this is so enticing, and this is so exciting! It's time for my breakfast feasting; it's time for celebrating.

Then his big alligator eyes started shining so bright, and his big alligator teeth were smiling with delight.

Now, the Little Red Chicken was standing at the edge of the water.
And the Big Alligator was swimming just around the corner.
He was splashing in the pond, bopping his big head up and down.
Waving his big, long tail, singing softly to himself, and dancing around.
"Mmmmh, yummy, yummy breakfast for my tummy."

"Wow, wow, super wow!
It's time to have my breakfast now.
Something nice and sweet for my tongue and teeth.
Something good to eat, it's always a special treat. Yummy, yummy! So delicious and tasty. Yummy, yummy, yummy for my tummy."

*The Big Alligator swam slowly toward the Little Red Chicken,
who was now pecking at the edge of the pond.
"Hi there, Little Red Chicken," said the Big Alligator.*

*"Hello there, Big Alligator," said the Little Red Chicken.
Now the Big Alligator was having fun,
talking to the Little Red Chicken in the morning sun.
"Hey, hey, what do you say? Do you want to swim in my pond today?"*

*The Little Red Chicken replied,
"No, no, I can't swim, and neither can I fly. I really want to go to the other side,
but this pond is too big and far too wide."*

"Why do you want to go to the other side of the pond? Can you tell me?"
The Big Alligator asked curiously, grinning and pretending to be friendly.

But the Little Red Chicken didn't give him an answer so quickly.
Gazing across the water, she smiled so shyly.
And she responded in a voice so gently. "Can you please help me
to cross the pond today, to go to the other side and play?"

"Sure, yes, of course, I can help you, Little Red Chicken;
today is your lucky day.
I can help you to cross the pond, and I can help you to find your way."
The Big Alligator replied with a funny smile on his face.
Grinning and waving his big, long tail and splashing water all over the place.

Thinking to himself, "Mmmmh, yummy, yummy breakfast for my tummy.
Wow, wow, super wow! It's time to have my breakfast now.
Something nice and sweet for my tongue and teeth.
Something good to eat, it's always a special treat.
Yummy, yummy, so delicious and tasty. Yummy, yummy,
yummy for my tummy."

The Big Alligator stretched out his mighty tail longer and longer,
like a bridge
for the Little Red Chicken to step up and walk across the water.
"Get on my back, Little Red Chicken," said the Big Alligator,
"Now that we are friends, we are no longer strangers.
I will give you a ride across the water. And I will protect you from danger."

The Little Red Chicken jumped up onto the huge tail of the Big Alligator and
said, "Are you going to eat me, Mr. Big Alligator?"

*The Big Alligator calmly answered, "Nooo, no, I am not hungry today.
I would never eat a beautiful Little Red Chicken like you anyway."
Grinning with his funny alligator smile and showing off his big alligator teeth.
But he was really sharpening his bite and getting ready to eat.*

*Thinking to himself all along, repeating the words to his favourite song;
"Mmmmh, yummy, yummy breakfast for my tummy.
Wow, wow, super wow! It's time to have my breakfast now.
Something nice and sweet for my tongue and teeth.
Something good to eat, it's always a special treat.
Yummy, yummy, so delicious and tasty. Yummy, yummy,
yummy for my tummy."*

The Little Red Chicken sat upon the back of the Big Alligator.
And they sailed off like explorers together across the waters.
In the middle of the pond, the Big Alligator looked up over his shoulder.
"Are you having fun up there, Little Red Chicken? Do you like the adventure?"
asked the Big Alligator.

"Yes, yes, I am having a very good time floating on top of the water.
It's dry and comfy up here,
and I can see everything so clear," the Little Red Chicken replied.

Then, the Big Alligator
started rolling and spinning around in the water.
Shaking up his mighty body like a rugged boat in stormy thunder!
Surprising the Little Red Chicken with a crazy game of danger.
But the Little Red Chicken kept on holding on, stronger and stronger.

The Big Alligator was rolling around faster and faster. He was hoping to throw off the Little Red Chicken and drop her in the water. To catch and snatch the Little Red Chicken for his breakfast appetizer.

Now, the Big Alligator was trying harder and harder.
But the Little Red Chicken ran faster and faster.
She moved her little chicken feet quicker and quicker.
Keeping up with the speed of the Big Alligator as he kept on turning around and around. Waving his big, long tail and splashing in the water.

It was a bumpy ride on the back of the Big Alligator. But the Little Red Chicken was still holding on stronger. She is a brave character with a joyful and playful nature. She kept on laughing along the way, enjoying the adventure.

*After a while, the Big Alligator became so tired
and so exhausted that he gave up because he could not keep up any longer.
But still, he really did not want to give up so easily.
His stomach was growling, and he was feeling very hungry.
Slowly but surely, he was getting really angry.
Somehow, he got to find a way to catch this Little Red Chicken today.*

*The Little Red Chicken shouted out loud.
"Hooray, hooray, hooray! This is so exciting, I must say.
I really like this game that we are playing today." The Big Alligator looked over
his shoulder again to say, "Oh yes, my little friend, it is always nice to swim
and play. It's nice to go sailing with me on a bright and sunny day."*

Now, the Little Red Chicken was jumping up and down.
Saying, "Thank you, Mr. Big Alligator, for being a good friend.
I love it when we splash and spin in the water around and around.
Oh yeah, oh yeah, that was so much fun. Let's do it again."

But it wasn't fun for the Big Alligator anymore.
He was too tired and too hungry, and now he wanted to settle the score. He was thinking about what next to do.
How can he find a way to make his breakfast dream come true?

*So, the Big Alligator
shook his big, long tail harder and harder. Splashing and spinning around faster and faster. Jumping up and down and diving under the water. Throwing the Little Red Chicken into a terrifying world of danger.*

*The Big Alligator dove down into the pond, deeper and deeper.
Leaving the Little Red Chicken all alone, floating in the water.
Worrying because she couldn't swim. And wondering how to save herself from danger. She remembered that Mommy always said, "Be careful of strangers."*

Suddenly, the Big Alligator jumped out from under the water. Shaking his big long tail, with his dragon eyes glowing like blazing fire!

Splashing and smashing the water and croaking loudly like a roaring thunder.

Powerful like a mystical creature in the wonderful world of nature!

The Big Alligator was spinning around and around.

Shaking up the water with his big, long tail.

He threw the Little Red Chicken way up in the air and said,

"Try and escape this time if you dare."

*Then the Big Alligator
opened up his gigantic mouth. His jaws were wide open,
with his huge body and his big sharp teeth showing.
Jumping up in the air, ready for the catch and shouting:
"Breakfast time, breakfast time.
Mmmmh, yummy, yummy breakfast for my tummy!"*

Thinking to himself all along, repeating the words to his favourite song.
"Mmmmh, yummy, yummy breakfast for my tummy."

"Wow, wow, super wow! It's time to have my breakfast now.
Something nice and sweet for my tongue and teeth.
Something good to eat, it's always a special treat.
Yummy, yummy, so delicious and tasty. Yummy, yummy,
yummy for my tummy."
But the Little Red Chicken did not cry; instead, she looked across the waters.

And she looked up high at the birds in the sky.
Then she started to spread her wings, And suddenly, she began to fly.
She flew and flew all the way to the other side of the pond.
Surprising the Big Alligator and herself.

"Wow, yeah, I can fly! I can fly! I made it!"
The Little Red Chicken shouted with joy and happiness.
"I can fly! I can fly! I made it to the other side!"

*As soon as her little chicken feet landed on dry land,
the Little Red Chicken started to sing a brand new song.
She was so happy-go-lucky, walking in the sand.
Dancing together with the other birds and singing her brand new song.*

*"Wow, wow, super wow! Look and see what I can do now.
I can spread my wings and fly like a bird up in the sky!
Yes, I can fly! I can fly! Like a bird up in the sky!
Oh yes, I can do it. Oh yes, I made it.
I can spread my wings with a new song to sing.
I can spread my wings and fly like a bird up in the sky."*

Meanwhile, the Big Alligator was very angry,
hungry and grumpy for not having his breakfast this morning.
But the Little Red Chicken was filled with joy and happiness.

She looked back at the Big Alligator and said,
"Thank you for helping me to cross the pond.
I had so much fun; what a great adventure!
But now I know why Mommy always says, "Be careful of strangers."
And I learned a big lesson today, 'Always look out for danger.'
So, bye-bye. I cannot stay with you today.
I am on my way to have some fun and play. See you later, Mr. Big Alligator."

To be continued........

The Little Red Chicken

&

The Big Alligator

Written by Gilroy Barrett &

Rasta Reuben Kwabena

Illustrated by Omar Taylor

About The Authors
(Gilroy Kirk Barrett)

Gilroy Kirk Barrett was born in Spanish Town Jamaica, in the Parish of St Catherine. From his early childhood years, he developed a great love and appreciation for music and songs and a great admiration for storybooks and storytelling. So, he decided to pursue his dream of having a successful career in the world of music and the performing arts.

Even though the road to success was rugged and challenging, nevertheless this would not stop Mr. Gilroy Barrett from holding on strong to his dream. He immersed himself in music, hoping his dream would lead the way forward to fulfilling his purpose in life. Along the way, he also developed a love for writing songs. And over the years, he expanded his expertise with the pen into other forms of creative writing such as writing short stories, children's stories, and movie scripts, etc.

He nourished his creative vision and his writing skills by travelling internationally and sojourning for multiple years in various countries. Moving from Jamaica to the Caribbean island of Curacao Netherlands Antilles. Eventually, Mr. Gilroy Barrett moved on to Ghana, the motherland of Africa, connecting deeper to his African roots and culture.

This also helped him to further develop his talents for writing lyrics and performing music. Soon, he was on the move again, sojourning, this time in Changsha, China, and Hong Kong, which became his new home for a while. After this, he also travelled to India for a concert performance and an extended visit of six months. During this time, he wrote new songs and new stories, networking together with various upcoming writers, artists and musicians from China and India.

This vibrant multicultural travel experience has helped the author and musician to meet many talented people from all around the world. Tremendously inspiring his worldview of One Love & Harmony for the family of humanity and respect for the natural mystical world of nature. Now, Mr. Gilroy Barrett is ready to share his international vision and his creative writing projects with the world at large. In this journey of dreams and destiny, of songwriting and storytelling. from the page to the stage.

Today, he lives mainly in Netherlands, from where he can network with Europe and Africa as well as with China and India. Across the Atlantic, he maintains strong connections to Jamaica and the USA, where he has many close relatives and friends. He credits both his beloved mother and his beloved grandmother for helping him to achieve success by being the major pillars of inspiration and guidance in his life.

About The Authors
(Rasta Reuben Kwabena)

Rasta Reuben Kwabena (aka George Phinn Jr) is a multi-talented artist, singer, songwriter, author, and music composer born in Kingston, Jamaica. GMV Global Muzik Village: Recording & Performing Artist, SELASSIE iPOWER Muzik aka Reggae Planet Ambassadors Worldwide.

The musical author is highly inspired by Rastafari culture and Reggae music and by the great vision of One Love. He is also motivated by the spiritual and cultural vibrations of his Jamaican & African ancient roots, heritage, and legacy.

Kwabena's love of music & singing and his spiritual inspiration were firstly inspired by his devoutly Christian grandmother, Ms. Amber Brown, in the churches of Jamaica. And by The Rastafarians, who also lived in the same tenement yard in Kingston, Jamaica, where he grew up with his family in his early childhood years.

His musical talent and his creative writing skills were also nurtured by his mother and father, who are devoted to collecting all types of good international music, particularly from the great Jamaican, Afro-Caribbean and Afro-American music scenes. Eventually, Rasta Reuben Kwabena immigrated from Kingston, Jamaica to

Toronto Ontario, Canada, with his Mom and Dad and brothers, and now currently resides in Vancouver, BC, Canada. However, he is also an avid international traveler who has travelled and sojourned in various regions of the world, from Jamaica to North America, to Australia, to Europe and to West Africa. This worldwide experience has further expanded his musical inspiration and his creative writing vision.

Rasta Reuben Kwabena (aka George Phinn Jr) started writing, composing, and arranging songs with his musical brothers, Frederick "Fredlocks Asher" Phinn and David "Uncle Dropsi" Phinn. Initially, he honed his craft at C. W. Jefferys Collegiate Institute in Toronto, Ontario, Canada. A very special school for the arts. This is where Kwabena studied the art of music, learned to play musical instruments, and studied creative writing, poetry, journalism, and theatre performing arts.

His father used to read Kwabena's early poems and recognized his son's natural talent for creative writing. Therefore, he instructed his son to attend this special high school collegiate to further his musical talent and writing skills. In the words of Rasta Reuben Kwabena, "C. W. Jefferys Collegiate Institute was a far distance from our home area. And it took a longer time to get there by bus. However, now I realize that I am forever grateful to my Dad for choosing that particular school for me because the curriculum was focused primarily on music, arts and literature and theatre."

"JAH gave me my Talent for music and creative writing as a Natural Gift. And combining creativity with education in that school greatly helped me to develop and nurture my natural talents, which I now share with the world at large."

About The Illustrator
(Omar Taylor)

Omar Taylor is an outstanding self-taught artist and illustrator, born in St Elizabeth, Jamaica. At the age of two, he moved to Waterford, Portmore, in the parish of St. Catherine. Soon thereafter, in his early childhood years, he discovered that he had an artistic gift at the young age of six.

"I was in the second grade at Waterford Primary School, and my teacher at the time, Mrs. Donaldson, asked the class to draw a cocoa plant from a book, which I did. And to the teacher's surprise, it was too good to be true for a six-year-old to draw. At first, she claimed that it was printed," recalled Omar.

However, upon further inspection, the teacher soon realized that the brilliantly illustrated drawing of the cocoa plant by Omar, was actually much bigger than the one which was pictured in the book. She recognized his artistic talent and said, "This is amazing; you clearly have a gift!" And that's how it all began.

Ever since that day, Omar Taylor has continued to further nurture and develop his talent with various levels of educational achievements as well as constantly working on several art projects.

He is fully devoted to his vision of becoming a worldwide recognized artist illustrator hoping that one day he will burst into the big time.

After leaving Waterford Primary, he attended Waterford Secondary, where he met art teachers Ms. Allen and Ms. Sterling. Both were amazed at his talent.

He completed secondary school with a distinction in arts and crafts, and then he enrolled at the Portmore Community College, where he did a course in business. He had to find ways of earning a living, so he started painting signs banners and promotional posters for businesses and events, etc.

"People always tried to persuade me to paint for a gallery," he pointed out. "So, I started exploring other forms of art like those which I had seen in the galleries, and I caught on very quickly. However, I came across tattooing and fell in love with it, and I took a break from painting for a while."

Omar Taylor views tattoos as a form of creative artwork and as a way to further expand his talent, to showcase his creative expertise and to express his artistic versatility. "Putting tattoos on people's skin is an art form which I love and the appreciation from my clients keeps me motivated.

On the other hand, in addition to my work with tattoos, painting is the other side of my talent, which only a few people know. And for this reason, I take this opportunity to show the other side of Omar," explains the artist illustrator.

The artist continues to grow and expand his creative vision. Stepping boldly into new frontiers of artistic expression, such as providing artwork illustrations for the world of literature, including children's storybooks, novels, comics, cartoons, etc. His creative artwork can be described as brilliant, eye-catching, imaginative, and compelling. Four of his special pieces include 'Great Minds', 'Brilliant Birds', 'Mother and Child' and 'Pattoo'. 'Brilliant Birds', in his mind, stands out because of its colours, while 'Pattoo' was an experience that came out "good."

Omar Taylor's inspiration comes from people such as Martin Luther King Jr. and the great legendary Jamaican reggae icon Robert 'Bob' Nesta Marley. He is also inspired by the beautiful tropical scenery of the Caribbean islands and by the people and circumstances in his life. And he admires the artwork of local artists Webster Campbell from Tavern, and Barrington Watson.

While travelling on a trip abroad some years ago, Omar stumbled on some paintings by Michelangelo, and this further pushed his creative mind to higher heights. "One day, I hope to have my own gallery. For now, I use social media to get my work out into the public domain," he said. The outstanding artist illustrator Omar Taylor is consistently hard at work with his art as he awaits the creation of his masterpiece, which will ultimately propel his name to international recognition and worldwide fame.

He continues his inspiring journey with the determination to succeed. Maintaining his inspiration and his creative vision to master his craft and fulfill his destiny. To nurture and expand his natural talent for artwork, which he now shares with the people in his community and with the families and children of the world.

The Little Red Chicken

&

The Big Alligator

Written by Gilroy Barrett &

Rasta Reuben Kwabena

Illustrated by Omar Taylor

www.ingramcontent.com/pod-product-compliance
Lightning Source LLC
Chambersburg PA
CBHW050740110526
44590CB00002B/38